Poems of Inspector Chen

Qiu Xiaolong

Introduction

The poems in the present collection are compiled chronologically, to be more specific, in the order of their appearance in the novels in the Inspector Chen series.

Less than half of the poems in the collection appear—either entirely or partially— in the novels, but even in case of entirety, the poems here may show small or substantial difference from those in the original versions. Chen writes in a hurry or under stress during the investigation, and as a rule, he takes time to revise and rewrite them later. Alternatively, some of the poems on the occasions of the novels could also have been written earlier, even in the days before he became an inspector.

Chen Cao started writing during his college years in the early eighties, a period sometimes described as "golden" for the modern Chinese poetry. After the ending of the Cultural Revolution in 1976, a considerable number of young people came passionately onto the literary scene. But Chen is more of an accidental poet. While majoring in English and American literature, he studied with the well-known poet and critic Bian Zhilin (1910-2000), and handed in several pieces written as a sort of homework. With Bian's encouragement,

Chen had them published in *Poetry* and other magazines. In the meantime, he started translating T. S. Eliot and other western poets, which added to his visibility in the circle. While doing research for his thesis on Eliot, he fell in love with a young librarian named Ling in Beijing Library. Some of his early poems turned out to be idealistic in spite of the modernist influence.

It did not take long for a different tone to be discernable in his lines. He parted with Ling after learning about her father being a powerful Politburo member at the top. He was concerned about loss of independence in the event of such a family alliance. Then, after college graduation, he was state-assigned to work at the Shanghai Police Bureau, an arrangement which was taken for granted in the then government policy: people were all supposed to work in the Party's interests regardless of the personal preference or pursuance.

He worked as an unwilling cop, initially, translating police procedures, composing political newsletter, doing all sorts of odd jobs for quite a while. His poems grew somber, for which he was viewed as a "Chinese modernist," a politically negative label. His enrollment as a member of the

Chinese Writers' Association helped little. Among his colleagues, he was seen as an unorthodox cop not dedicated to the real job.

But another surprising turn intervened. The Party's new cadre promotion policy came with an unprecedented emphasis on a candidate's educational credentials, thanks to which, Chen was chosen. The whispered speculation about his off-and-on contact with Ling played into his favor as well. He was admitted into the Party, given real cases, and swept into a rapid rise in the bureau. As the head of the Special Case Squad, Chen was fortunate enough to find a capable partner and close friend in Detective Yut. In the early nineties, Chen was made the chief inspector of the Shanghai Police Bureau. From then on, his investigations are represented in the nine novels so far in the Inspector Chen series.

Notwithstanding the strenuous caseload, he finds the police work widening the range of the poetry subject matter for him, triggering off lines in response to the unimaginable cruelties, irrationalities, corruptions, insanities as revealed in investigation. In *A Loyal Character Dancer*, he comes to the crucial clue through a poem in the background of the educated youth movement; in *The Case of Two Cities*, a Prufrock-like parody helps to throw light on his predicament as a Party member cop; in *Red Mandarin Dress*, studies of the comparative poetics lends insight into the complicated case; in *Don't Cry, Tai Lake*, examining the pollution of the nature as well as of the human nature prompts Chen into a sequence with a spatial structure... In each and every Inspector Chen novel, poems are produced or recollected in spite of himself.

Chen develops some of his stylistic features through the police work too. In *When Red Is Black*, he comes across an incomplete manuscript of classical Chinese poetry translation by an intellectual murdered during the Cultural Revolution. To keep his pledge to the dead, Chen edits the ms. with some of his own translation and has it published. Inspired in the process of it, he also introduces into his own poems a sort of dialogue with the Tang and Song masters, carrying on a comparison and contrast between the ancient and the present-day China, and sometimes having the original juxtaposed with his lines in correspondence.

In his line of duty, Inspector Chen has to walk a lot, observing, canvassing, and thinking, around the city of Shanghai, particularly in the old sections of the *shikumen* houses and narrow lanes, coming upon not just the clues for investigation, but also much for reflection as an independent-thinking intellectual. He jots down fragments in a small notebook, like the Tang dynasty poet Li He who rode around on a donkey, dashing off the lines whenever obtainable, and dropping them into a cloth bag for composition later. That adds a touch of "found poetry" to Chen's work.

In the meantime, poetry proves specially meaningful for Inspector Chen in an unexpected way. It is not enough, as he always believes, to merely focus on whodunit; it is imperative for him to reach a comprehensive understanding of the social, cultural and historical circumstances in which crimes and tragedies take place. With the Party's interest above everything else—above law—in the one-Party system, he cannot but face the dire politics involved in investigations, staring long and frequent into the abyss which stares back. No way of solving the conflict between a conscientious cop and a Party cadre, poetry-writing serves for him like a temporary escape from the mounting frustrations. He compares the momentary break to the Song dynasty poet Su Shi's metaphor about staying on the moon, much higher, but also much too cold to stay for long, though a necessary change for the moment. Furthermore, a poetic perspective, so to speak, in addition yet also in contradiction to the political perspective imposed on Chen. The juxtaposition keeps him from identifying himself with the authoritarian system, so that he may sees things from a much-needed distance.

His rise in the Party system brings about change in his experience as a poet. As an executive member of the Chinese Writers' Association, he is often chosen as a Chinese representative to meet with western poets and writers, and on one occasions, to lead the Chinese Writers' Delegation abroad, as in *The Case of Two Cities*. Chen has a poetry collection published, but he soon discovers that it is done through a large amount paid by a Big Buck associate in secret, something done for his favor in the omnipresent cobweb of connections in China. It comes as a terrible blow to his conviction about the relevance of poetry in today's society.

During the period, changes also occur in his personal life. Like in a proverb, however, things go the wrong way eight or nine times out of ten, which cannot but somewhat inform his poems. But a follower of Eliot's "impersonal theory," he insists on separating the man who suffers from the poet who writes. In that, Chen also benefits from a tradition in the classical Chinese poetics, in which love poems are read as political allegories through the persona of a unrequited lover. For instance, "untitled poems" by Li Shangyin, one of Chen's favorite Tang dynasty poets, are often interpreted like that, the way John Donne's love poems are read for the metaphysical significance.

Along with the spectacular economic transformation in China, the literary scene too is changing dramatically. Not like in the early eighties, instead of being fashionable or politically meaningful with the authoritarian government persecution for any independent voice, a poet like Chen becomes marginalized. In the increasingly materialistic society, less and less readers have the time or interests for poetry. People no longer take it seriously. Even with occasional publishing still possible here and there, it's more like decoration than anything else.

But with so much happening in the contemporary Chinese society, Inspector Chen has no choice but to continues investigating, and writing too, even though a more cynical and disillusioned cop and poet. He still remembers what his later father told him, quoting Confucius, "Knowing it's impractical—almost impossible to do it, you still have to do what you should do."

Contents

The Open Country and the Sea

I would not be the dainty key-ring on your finger,

nor the seaweed-mantled obsidian you'd lean on.

So I shaped you into a delicate vase in my gaze,

and in your mouth placed fresh carnations.

Simply because of your white graceful neck

I captured the color and form of my dream.

One morning I found myself turned into water,

with neither motion nor gesture nor expression.

"Now that it smells," you asked me,

"shouldn't we change it?"

In the night, you dreamed

of the open country, and I, of the sea.

* In his college years, Chen was passionately into

existentialism. He wrote the poem while reading Sartre's

Being and Nothingness.

Birthday Night

3:30 A.M. A dog barking

against the moon-bleached night...

Is the dog barking into my dream

or am I dreaming into the dog?

Justification

A withered tree proves to be

ideal for the termites, which

legitimate the noise of

a philosopher-billed woodpecker

deep in the woods, where

a henpecked hunter skulks

in dread of his wife,

half-heartedly raising his gun.

Once, a comrade lectured me

on politics and logic, her

bare shoulder rippling

under my palm: "Do what

you want; you are always able

to find reasons later."

An apple rolled out the picnic hamper.

Snatches of a *pipa* melody drifted

from a blue boat. I lost myself

in her cascading hair, which

smelled of barbecued ribs.

Comparative Poetics

It takes the fall of a city

for Bai and Fan to fall in love,

and the studies of William Emption

for me to study Guan Daoshen's lines

about how to make a pottery

of the mixed Oriental and Occidental.

Out of the same chunk

of clay, shape a you,

shape a me. Crush us

both into clay again, mix

it with water, reshape

a you, reshape a me.

So, I have you in my body,

and you'll have me forever in yours, too.

* Bai and Fan are the lovers in the story "Love with the Fall of the City" by Eileen Chang, and Chen came upon Guan Daoshn's poem (in the Italic) when he read William Empson's raving about it in a comparative literature seminar. Guan (1262-

1319) was a brilliant painter, calligrapher, and poet in the Song
dynasty.

Today

Not because of the frozen memories

of yesterday, not because

of the budding expectations

for tomorrow, we are throwing

ourselves into today.

Consumed with yesterday's regrets,

life is nothing but a sigh

in the dream, contented

with the fantasies for tomorrow,

life yawns into a dream.

After all, where is life

except in today?

* Stephen Spender (1909-1995) visited China in 1981. Chen was chosen as a young representative poet to meet with the British poet during his stay in Beijing. Chen read the poem titled "Today," which was later included in *China Diary* by Stephen Spender and David Hockney, in a version slightly different through translation.

After Fragment

You are looking out of the lane

at the scene, and tourists,

looking back at you

for the scene of the lane.

The setting sun silhouettes you

against the decayed wall

of the lane, you silhouette

the memories of the lane.

* The poem is in imitation of "Fragment" by Bian Zhilin
(1910-2000), a modern Chinese poet, Chen studied with him
in Beijing in his college years. Bian's original poem also
appears in *Death of a Red Heroine*.

Stamp

Your father collected stamps, cutting

days and nights to small squares,

soaking a sky full of them

in a wash basin, and drying them

on the doors, windows, and mirrors:

two stamps in his eyes,

the face, an unfamiliar envelope,

the world, an unfolding album.

You, too, was glued onto the white

immaculate background with a message

in each fleeting snowflake. Overnight,

a crane's footprints disappeared.

Mailed to a non-existent address

to obtain a postmark, you was not

returned, by mistake, as occasionally

happens, at the post office.

To a Friend Who Reads Lacan

The bookmark puts you among the pages

where you wish to forget.

What is imaginable, but not innocent.

Looking out the window, you see

a *tung*-oiled paper umbrella,

red-pointed,

unfolded on the porch,

round as a gigantic breast

swaying in the wind.

You occupy the chair as the sight

of its shapely arms occupies your mind.

In the valley, the echo tries bringing

itself to face what it is not.

The Lunar Lumberjack

Under the cold eye of the earth

I am an absurdity

hacking on like possessed,

chopping days, slashing nights,

hewing years, millions

of years, yellow leaves piling up

like the pages of the histories

wood-crumbs filling my nostrils

till I can barely breathe.

Cringing at the inevitable,

gasping for the insubstantial,

lunar air, the gash

appears always on the verge

of uttering a final cry, like

my own as the steadily

bending tree springs up again,

refreshed as ever, glaring

with its acrid crumbs burning

my nostrils and my lungs

while the supercilious stars

regard me from the afar.

Yet I raise the ax once more

hacking desire, hacking despair,

a dark, passionate torrent

pouring from my beard

into the sand, for it's only

in this too familiar clamor,

I know I exist, wielding

my ax against the sickness,

belonging to a legend

that does not belong to me.

* According to an ancient Chinese legend, Wu Gang is doomed to the never-ending labor on the moon of chopping down an osmanthus tree, which always stands up again the moment it is almost felled. It is another poem written during Chen's "existentialist period."

Gargoyle

It was on a hillside, Jingshan, Forbidden City,

where the Qing Emperors had succeeded

the Ming Emperors. There we sat

on a slab of rock, watching

the evening spreading out

against the glazed eaves

of the splendid palace. Beneath us,

waves of buses kept flowing

along the Huangchen Road (a moat,

originally, hundreds of years earlier).

We murmured words in Chinese,

then in English we were learning.

The bronze stork, which had watched

the Qing Dowager, was still starring

ahead. You dreamed of us,

you said, becoming two gargoyles

gurgling at *Yangxing* imperial hall

all night long, babbling in words

comprehensible only to ourselves.

A mist enveloping the hill, we rose

to see a tree with a white board

saying, "It's on this very tree

that Emperor Chongzhen hung himself,"

I shivered at the sign's resemblance

to the blackboard hung by Red Guards

round my father's neck

in the Cultural Revolution.

In a bat-woven evening draft

from the end of the somber park trail

I felt your bare arm so chilly

with the sight of a limo waiting there for you,

dispatched from your family

in the Central South Sea,

the present-day Forbidden City.

Of a sudden, the gargoyle

behind us seemed to be

gurgling out a decision

understandable only to me.

* The Central South Sea, once part of the Forbidden City, is

nowadays the complex where the top Party and government

24

leaders live and work. Chen parted with Ling after learning about her father being a Politburo member at the top, a decision made at the moment he realized the difference in the family background.

In the Attic

At the scream of a siren in the depth of the night

my little tape begins to play.

I am peeling an apple: the window

frames nothing but a concept of free fall.

The world is suddener than we imagine—

under the knife, over an on-off switch

The golden clock that Venus bears aloft

has inexplicably stopped.

Kuawu, the god of thirst, still chases the sun

across the crumbling wall.

* After college graduation, Chen was assigned to work
at the Shanghai Police Bureau. Because of the housing
shortage of the city, he stayed with his mother in an
attic for several years. He did not get his own apartment
until in the early nineties, as in *Death of a Red Heroine*.

Postwoman

The rain has soaked

your shoulder-length hair

light green, reflecting

from your uniform,

with the mails, like spring

white blossom bursting

from your arms, reaching

into the neighboring windows--

"Here you are!"

And through the windows

laughter flies out, perching

on the verdant branches

around you, savoring

the plums of your dimples,

as you pass, your arms

hung down, listless, as usual,

by my opened door.

* As a rising Party-member official, Chen feels obliged, occasionally, to write something politically correct, for instance, to sing the praise of the working class people, though "Postwoman" is more about his own experience of waiting for the letter from Beijing. Part of the poem appears in *Death of a Red Heroin.*

Eight Years Ago

That January morning I awoke

to your black hair tumbling

against a snow-blanked

world, an owl's doubtful eyes blinking

in the clock, a poster of a blue jay

bearing an orange of the sun

along the wall. A word

burbled you, breaking

the day.

A word is a bird:

It perches, then flies.

* Years after his parting with Ling, Chen remembers a poster in
her bedroom, and some words she murmured that morning. The
poster shows a blue jay carrying the sun on its back with the
caption underneath: "What will come eventually comes." Part of
the poems appears in *Death of a Red Heroine*.

Night Talk

Creamy coffee cold,

toy bricks of sugar cubes

crumbling, a butter blossom still

reminiscent of freedom

on the mutilated cake,

the knife aside, like

a footnote. It is said

some people can tell the time

by the change of color

in a cat's eyes—but you can't.

Doubt, a heap of ancient dregs

from the bottle of *Great Wall*

rests in the sparkling wine.

Under the play of neon lights

the Uygur girl on the wall

is carrying grapes to you,

infinite motion, light

as a summer in grateful tears

when a bit of the golden paint,

under her bangled bare feet,

flakes from the frame around her.

Nothing appears more accidental

than the world in words.

A rubric turns by chance

in your hands, and the result,

like any result, is called history.

Through the window we see no star.

Mind's square appears deserted,

not a pennant left. Only a rag picker

of the time passes by, dropping scraps

of every minute into her basket.

* For years, poems and novels were given unjustified political

interpretations in China. In 1962, Mao made the statement about

the novel *Liu Zhidan*. "It is a big invention to launch an attack

against the Party with a novel." That immediately brought down

Xi Zhongxun (the father of the current Chinese President Xi

Jinpin) from his then position as a Vice Premier. In *Death of a*

Red Heroine, an old official Commissar Zhang in the

Shanghai Police Bureau finds fault with Chen's poems "Night Talk" published after the crackdown of the student movement in the Tiananmen Square in 1989. The mentioning of the square and gun in the poem proves to be enough for Zhang to write a report to alert the higher authorities, accusing Chen of being in sympathy with the students, but not in solidarity with the Party.

For Poet M. L. Rosenthal

Whatever it is, it has to have

the monomania of a mule,

to circle, blindfolded,

the stone mill, dragging the weight

its back can possibly endure.

Whatever comes out of the drudgery

will not come to its muzzled mouth—

the world, when finally seen

without the black cloth,

is a muddled mishap.

* Chen dedicated this poem to M. L. Rosenthal
(1917-1996), whom Chen met as a representative of
the Shanghai during the American poet's visit to
China, as described in *Death of a Red Heroine*. The
poem is based on a common scene of a blindfolded
mule pulling at a stone mill in the Chinese
countryside.

Translating Ma Zhiyuan

Withered vines, old trees, crows at dusk,

a small bridge over the flowing water, a few houses,

an ancient path, the west wind, a lean horse,

and the sun setting...

A heart-broken traveler at the end of the world.

You have left all the nouns

without any conjunctions or verbs

for me to put them together

like building blocks, in another

language, in another land,

and the moon setting…

A heartless keyboard at the end of its wits.

* Ma Zhiyuan (1250-1321), a Yuan dynasty poet.

Yu Dafu

In 1942, three years before the ending

of the Anti-Japanese War, after the fall

of Hong Kong, his wife's divorce, and

the tabloid typhoon, Dafu left China,

incognito, to an Indonesian isle, where

he called himself "Zhao, the black-bearded,"

started a small rice shop, and bought

a native girl, thirty years younger,

at the price of an "untouched,"

who could not speak his language.

A gigantic ledger opened him

in the morning, figures moved him up

and down a mahogany abacus, until

the curfew closed him in her arms,

like in a sack of soft darkness:

time was streaming in a handful

of rice—*look, white-&-fancy*—

steaming through his fingers.

A chewed betel nut stuck on the counter.

He quit holding himself like

a balloon against a horizon

ablaze with cigarette butts.

One midnight he was startled awake,

with the leaves shivering,

inexplicably, against the window.

She grasped at the mosquito net

in her sleep. A gold fish

jumped out, dancing furiously

on the ground. Wordless,

a young woman's capability

of featuring jealousy

in incorrigibly plural correspondence

of the world illuminated him.

It must have been another man,

dead long before, who had said:

The limits of his language

are the limits of his possibility.

All night he wrote her

with his tongue, nose tip, and beard.

Eventually, his biographers claim all

this as a camouflage, necessary

for the resistance activities

against Japan. And they come

to her, like tired travelers

to a deserted monastery.

                    Her teeth

black from betel-nut-chewing,

a habit which husband has left

her, she forgets. She

has married several times.

Wriggling her toes like

cracked plastic petals, she

succeeds in bringing back

to her mind nothing except

the sensation of his big beard

tingling between her thighs.

* Yu Dafu (1896-1945), a modern Chinese poet, known for his

poems as well as his romantic affairs. During the anti-Japanese

war, he went incognito to Indonesia, where he settled down,

married a native girl about thirty years younger, who could not speak a single word in Chinese. It was a Gaugin-like mystery with a variety of interpretations. Anyway, he stayed with her there until his death shrouded in another mystery at the end of the war. In *A Loyal Character Dancer*, Inspector Chen shows to Inspector Rohn the poem based on Dafu's life. Chen likes Dafu's poems, particularly a romantic couplet. Chen had it copied on his folding fan, "Drunk, I whipped a superb horse so relentlessly, / I'm afraid of sentimentally dragging a beauty again!"

The Sunlight Burning Gold

The sunlight burning gold,

we cannot collect the day

from the ancient garden

into an album of old.

Let's pick our play,

or time will not pardon.

When all is told,

we cannot tell

the question from the answer.

Which is to hold

us under a spell,

the dance or the dancer?

Sad it's no longer sad,

the heart hardened anew,

not expecting pardon,

but grateful, and glad

to have been with you,

the sunlight lost on the garden.

* The poem appears in *A Loyal Character Dancer*. Inspector Chen and American Inspector Catherine Rohn join force in an international illegal immigration investigation, during which the two get attracted to each other. As a rising Party cadre, however, Chen knows an affair between them is unthinkable. In a Suzhou garden, he shows Catherine the lines based on Louis MaCneice's "The Sunlight on the Garden," in the tradition of expressing the inexpressible through a poem, which also passes as a comment on the other ill-starred lovers involved in the investigation.

Apologies to Zhang Ji

The moon setting, the crow cawing, the frost spreading out

against the sky, the maple trees, and the fisherman's light

moving across the river, someone still there, sleeping

in worries . By the Cold Mountain Temple

out of Gu Su City, the arrival

of a sampan in the midnight bells.

I come on a humid summer day

saturated with the construction noises

to catch a glimpse of the Tang poem

carved in gold on a black stone tablet,

and then to take a picture in front

of it, flashing a fictional smile like

other tourists—"That's all about it."

Crows, too languid to cry, sweating

under the scorching sun.

* Zhang Ji (715-779), a Tang dynasty poet, is

especially known for the poem "Mooring by the

Maple Bridge at Night" with its montage-like juxtaposition of scenes (in the Italic). Nowadays, the Cold Mountain Temple in Suzhou is a must-see tourist attraction because of the poem, though the scenes described in those lines are mostly gone. Suzhou is one of the favorite cities for Inspector Chen.

Finger Polishing

We are talking in a jammed workshop

picking our way, and our words,

amid the prizes, the gold-plated statuettes

staring at the circling flies. "The stuff

for your newspaper report: miracle made

by Chinese workers ," the director says.

"In Europe, special grinders alone

can do the job, but our workers finger-

polish the precision part."

Beside us, a group of women bending

over the work, their fingers shuttling

the ghastly fluorescent light.

My camera falls focusing

on a pale, middle-aged woman,

in her black threadbare homespun

vest soaked in sweat.

Summer heat overwhelms.

Zooming in, I'm shocked to see myself

galvanized into the shiny steel part

touched by Lili's fingertips,

soft yet solid

as an exotic grinder.

                    Not that

Lili really touched me. Not she, the prettiest

leftist. July, 1972, we were leaving,

an enthusiastic group of "the educated youths,"*

leaving for the countryside, "oh,

to be re-re-re-educated by

the po-or and lo-lo-wer middle

class peasants!" Chairman Mao's voice

screeched from a scratched record

at the station. By the locomotive Lili

burst into a dance, flourishing

a red paper heart she had cut, a miracle

in the design of a girl and a boy

holding the Chinese ideogram—"*loyalty*"

to Chairman Mao. Spring

of the Cultural Revolution breezed

through her fingers. Her hair streamed

into the dark eye of the sun.

A leap, her skirt

in a blossom, and the heart

jumped out of her hand, fluttering

like a flushed bird. A slip—

I rushed to its rescue, when she

caught it—just a finishing touch

to her performance. The people

roared out. I froze. She took my hand,

waving, our fingers branching

into each other, as if my blunder

were a much rehearsed act,

as if the curtain fell

against a piece of white paper

to set off the red heart, in which

I was the boy, she, the girl.

                          "The best fingers,"

the director keeps me nodding. It's she.

No mistake. But what? I can say,

of course, the most convenient words

to myself, that things change, like

in a proverb, as dramatically

as azure seas into mulberry fields, or

that all these years vanish—a flick

of your cigar. Here she is, changed

yet unchanged, her fingers

lathered in the greenish abrasive,

like bamboo shoots long immersed

in icy water, peeling, but

perfecting. She raises her hand, only

for once, to wipe the sweat

on her forehead, leaving

a phosphorescent trail. She

does not know me--not even

with the *Beijing Daily's* reporter

name label on my bosom.

                    "No story,"

the director says. "One of the millions

of the educated youths, she has become

'a poor-lower-middle class peasant' herself,

her fingers—tough as a grinder,

but a revolutionary one, polishing up

the spirit of our society, speaking

volumes of our socialism's superiority."

So came a central metaphor

for my report.

An emerald snail

crawls along the white wall.

* During the Cultural Revolution (1966-1976), China's

middle school graduates were called "educated youths,"

so it was necessary for them to "be re-educated by the

poor and lower middle class peasants" in the

countryside. The nationwide movement launched by

Mao was to get rid of the Red Guard students who had

served his need in the earlier power struggle, and in

response to his call, millions of young people left the

cities to reform themselves, physically as well as

spiritually, after the "poor and lower middle class

peasants." Some of them succeeded in such

transformation. In *A Loyal Character Dance*, the poem

tells a tragic love story, and it also provides a crucial

clue to the case investigated by Inspector Chen.

Journey

You keep on murmuring the name

of each new platform

each time the train slows

down, as if anxious to reorient

yourself along an unchanging isle

with ever-changing feet

in black loafers, wooden slippers,

shiny boots, muddy sandals...

Destination is not

on the unfolded map, nor

in the punched tickets, but

redefined, inevitably, the moment

it is reached, with the travelers

shaking off the dust there

into the dust here. Here is

never where you want to be.

Snow falls in the evening.

You turn to a shimmering light

on the window, a fly circling

its corner. Whenever you

raise your hand, it drones away—

only to return buzzing

to the same spot, inexplicably, like

a half-forgotten slogan echoing

from a long-ago revolution.

Overnight, the land appears

buried in white. Breathing hard

against the pane, you try to wipe

the vapor away, when you see

the window frame your ever-returning

reflection—like a fly.

Snowman

You have to be a snowman

to stand in the snow, listening

to the same message of the wind

with imperturbable patience, gazing

at the unchangeable scene, trying

not to lose yourself in the setting

while a hungry, homeless crow

starts to peck your red nose,

apparently, of a carrot.

*Chen "discovers" the poem by late Professor Yang in *When Red Is Black.*

A Transitional Cathay Image

The past is already past,

the future is still

in the future.

Here and now,

a clothes-tree is waiting, hung

with expectations, old-fashioned

or up-to-the-minute, brass buttons

solemnly gleaming, a low-cut

neckline, a damask butterfly

hovering at the bosom, or

an ostrich plume trembling.

All may come alive, suddenly,

vivid, vivacious in a draft

through the long empty corridor.

Red-clad, red-capped, a bellboy

smiles in a tall mirror,

drowsily as ever

by a silent stairway.

About Wang Changling

The chilly rain keeps falling

all night long into the Wu River...

At dawn, you are saying farewell

to your friend against the suddenly

solitary Wu mountains.

"When old folks and friends ask

about me at home, tell them:

'A ice-pure heart, a crystal vase.'"

I am the one you left

over a thousand years ago,

still traveling across mountains

and rivers, repeating, still repeating

the mystery of your message

far from home.

*Wang Changling (698-756), a well-known Tang dynasty poet.

Trying to Quote Su Shi

When you wonder at the possibility of waking

out of the endless cycle of old joy,

new grief, the waning moon hanging on

the sparse *tung* twigs, when an apparition

of a solitary wild goose wanders

like a hermit, trying each of the chilly boughs,

choosing not one to perch itself on,

the maple leaves falling cold

into the Wu river, when you envision

a moment years later of someone else

sighing over your life story, and pacing

here, with the same yellow pavilion

silhouetted against the night, when

you stand alone, unaware of the shadow

of the locust tree folding

into dawn, and of the time flowing

like water in the dark, the moon waning

and waxing with the people in reunion,

in separation...

There is no self to claim, I echo

your murmuring, amidst the cares

of the world, the night deep, the wind still,

no ripples in time's river.

* Su Shi (1037-1101), a Song dynasty poet as well as a statesman, whose work sometimes embodies an incredible amalgamation of Confucianism, Daoism, and Buddhism. Su Shi's poems, or part of them, appear frequently in Inspector Chen novels.

Mahjong Game

There is nothing but in interpretation.

In Chinese, a mahjong game is called

a square-city-war, with mahjong pieces

aligned like bricks, and connected,

eventually, into walls on four sides,

battles raging around...Cities built, cities

fallen, and cities rebuilt, like

strenuous repetitions of history.

The world presents itself in a game

of winning and losing. What means

means, if at all, only here

and now. Then the mahjong pieces

shuffle the players. As always,

hope is waiting anew

under their finger tips.

A Cricket's Song

How long ago was Li Bai moved

by his friend's song when

leaving, an autumn morning

by the Peach Blossom Lake,

a solitary sampan sailing

into the ceaselessly warring clouds

of the mid-Tang dynasty?

The wind that breaks a petal

breaks me.

       By Suzhou Creek, April's

cruelest fingers are fastening

a cricket of me screeching

against a rusted hook to catch

a rippling image of your

leaving, all your lectures

undelivered. Yuanlu,

do you hear me singing

by scratching my broken wings

at Shanghai Pudong Airport?

* Li Bai (701-762) wrote a well-known poem for his friend Cui Lun who came to see him off by the Peach Blossom Lake with a joyful song.

The Decision Night

Missing the midnight bus that passed

by the hotel, you headed back,

debating with yourself whether to leave

or not, amidst the leaves falling

like the bamboo slips for divination

in an ancient temple, darkly

portentous. The streets stretched on

like a tedious argument until

the entrance of Ninghai Food Market

greeted you with a long line of baskets—

plastic, bamboo, rattan, wood, straw—

of all shapes and sizes, leading

to a stall with a cardboard sign

of *yellow croaker,* a fish so popular

in Shanghai, the baskets there

stood for the virtuous wives who

would soon come, picking up the positions

in the line, their eyes still dreamy

with husbands' satisfaction...Bang,

bang, bang, a night worker was cracking

a gigantic frozen bar of the fish,

faceless in an upturned collar

of the cotton-padded overcoat

when you recognized

yourself reaching out in the handle

of a straw-bound basket in the line

embracing the night.

The decision was made for you.

* Until Deng Xiaoping decided to further the economic reform
in the late eighties, the food supply remained as a big problem
in the cities like Shanghai, hence the scene of the food market
as described in the poem.

Song after Prufrock

Shall I go, shall I go

with my Chinese accent and a roast

Peking duck, to her home

when the evening is spreading out

like a gigantic invitation poster

against the clouds of doubt?

I walk across the Loop, where

a blond girl hums a little air,

her shoulder-length hair flowing,

lighting the somber wall, singing,

her bare toes tapping on a bronze

plaque dedicated to Eliot,

in an evening redolent of songs.

Am I not being an idiot?

My necktie inserted by a pin,

my alligator leather shoes shining.

(They will think: "How yellow his skin!")

What will they say—to my quoting

from Shakespeare, Donne, and Hopkins?

In short, I am not sure.

(They will say: "But how strong his accent!")

Would it be worthwhile

to bite a Big Mac with a smile,

to squeeze the differences and all

into a small Ping-Pang ball,

to dream of her white teeth

nibbling at the cheddar cheese,

with a mud-covered toad

against a white swan on the road?

Should I explain a Chinese joke

with the help of an English book—

after baseball, chips and dips

and helpless tongue slips,

after deconstructing the character "ai

into radicals—*heart, water, friend* and *eye*,

after the pallid sleepless stress

smoothed by her golden tress

on the rug of a blossoming iron tree,

after turning on the TV,

not understanding why

those actors laugh and cry.

It's impossible to say

what I want to say!

What if she, kicking

off her sandals, trimming

her toenails, should say,

"That is not it at all,

not what I mean, at all."

Is it her red-painted toenail

that make me so frail?

Then how should I begin

to spin out all the butt-ends

of my days and ways

and how shall I pray and pay?

I should be a dragon yellow-glazed

along the wall of the forever-praised

Forbidden City. I'm no Li Bai

drowning in a cup of sighs,

but a chained monkey gesticulating,

with the name label shining

on the bosom of a Tang vest.

In short, I am not sure,

walking along a twilight-flooded beach.

I have seen the mermaids dancing

on TV, beyond reach,

beyond the reality's pinching.

I don't think that, singing on the sea,

they will shed their tails for me.

* Even in the days before Chen became a chief inspector, people had suggested that he pursue a career out of China. Disgusted with the politics in the one-Party system, Chen thinks about the possibility of studying abroad, particularly in the company of Catherine Rohn, an American police officer in a joint investigation in *A Loyal Character Dancer*, but a man of contradictions, Chen does not make the step. The thought comes to him again in *A Case of Two Cities*. During a trip to the States as a member of a Chinese writers' delegation secretly engaged in an anti-corruption investigation, he comes to St. Louis, where he gets the help from Catherine. Before leaving, he pays her a visit.

She is not at home, so he waits in a cafe nearby, thinking, and writing the poem. Although a decisive police officer unafraid of taking risks, Chen could be Prufrock-like in his personal life. The poem is also written as a tribute to T. S. Eliot in the poet's home city.

Neighborhood Phone Station

All the possibilities imaginable

of a postmarked phoenix.

There's nothing like

taking things for granted.

To make a phone call now,

for instance, you simply touch

a number in car, on bed, anywhere,

anytime. But that long-ago

Sunday morning, near the entrance

of Red Dust Lane, we were

standing in a long line, half-circling

the public phone station. The sun

radiated patience. A fungus

began appearing out of a cranny

in the lane wall when you turned

to the subject of existentialism.

One is made, I agreed,

by the decisions made

of free will. We came

to settle on a list of the people

we were going to invite

for an attic party. Finally reaching

the window of the phone station,

you found the line busy, and tried

two or three more times, in vain.

The queue quivered behind us

into an impatient question mark.

You dialed another number.

It got through. Another (who

now is your virtuous wife)

climbed up the attic that night

carrying your favorite

pine nut cake, her arms full,

her hair wet.

Give her my regards.

* Until the late eighties, most Shanghai people did not

have phones at home. They had to use neighborhood

phone service, usually in a "station" with two phones,

one to call out, and the other to call in, along with a

mobile operator to inform the recipient through a loud

speaker. It could quite a while for a call to go through,

with people waiting in a long line outside the station.

Alarm Clock

A bell rang urgently

on the platform, as if

the curtain had risen, as if

I had entered a familiar role

in the spotlight, putting

a hand on my heart, as if

a declaration, much rehearsed,

of affection that would reach out

across seas, across mountains

had carried a bouquet of me

to the vase at your window

of the Shanghai-Beijing express,

the way dawn carries

an alarm clock, and

you stamped your feet.

The anchorman cracks

his alarm clock in a nightmare

in *Groundhog Day*. The language

of weather forecasts, he realizes,

has cast him, morning

after morning. Here,

out the Daguangming Cinema,

an apple tree again

in wild blossom, regardless

of all the elapsed years: *The number is*

disconnected, no further information

available. No one hears

the bell ringing at the other end

of the line. It does not

need seas and mountains

to reach oblivion. When

an occasional siren sounds

in the distance, I miss the way

you stamp your feet.

Fish Tale

Here we are, *big bucks* in a dry month,

in a sampan-shaped saloon, where a young waitress

recommends the chef's special, "Qianlong's carp

with its eyes still turning on a platter—"

While travelling incognito in the south,

Emperor Qianlong boarded a sampan

on a stormy night, wet, cold, hungry

as a wolf. A fishing girl tried to fry the carp

too large for the wok, leaving its head

and tail stuck out of the sizzling oil.

Under the shadowy tung-oiled awning,

the fish tasted extraordinary tender,

its eyes goggling once in the dark—

Or was it something he imagined

with too much to drink?

Then the fish appeared as if

turning, magically, into the girl

bleeding, thrashing under him,

when he fell to suckling

her small toe like a dainty ball

of the live carp cheek.

"A legendary special," the waitress

serves the carp with its eyes turning

into the fishing girl, her feet bare,

silver-bangled, lighting the red carpet.

* The special dish appears in a couple of Inspector

Chen novels.

Red Mandarin Dress

Mother, I have tried to make the far-off echo

yield a clue to what is happening to me:

in the old mansion people come and go,

seeing only what they want to see.

The recall of the red mandarin dress

wears me out, flashing in the flowers,

your bare feet, your soft hand: the stress

of memory strips me of waking hours.

But we are flattened, framed in the zoom

of one moment—click—when cloud and rain

approaching fast, a doomful gloom

scurries across the horizon again.

Oh that is all I know, all I see.

Mother, you drink the cup for me.

* This is another poem Inspector Chen "discovers" in an

investigation in *Red Mandarin Dress*.

An Inspector's Round

Crumpling the draft, I step back into the role

shadowed by the surrounding skyscrapers.

In vain, I try to make the report

yield a clue to the bell for the city.

All that I know: what makes a cop

makes me. I patrol the surviving old lanes

and shabby streets, the scenes once familiar

in memories: a couple snuggling like

paper-cut on the door, a loaner connecting

cigarettes into an antenna, a granny bending

over a chamber pot in her bound feet like

broken twigs, a peddler hawking out of debris

like a suspect... A sign of *"demolition"*

deconstructs me. Nothing can avert the coming

of a bulldozer. It is not an easy task to push,

amidst the debris, the round to an end.

Li Shangyin's English Version I

The tenderness of the tea leaf between her lips.

Everything is possible, but not pardonable.

Propped up against a couple of pillows,

I am studying an English version

of Li Shangyin's poem. It is strange

to find a rich allusion transformed

into a cliché, as if undressed,

unimaginative in nakedness.

Still it puzzles me that in his poems,

love always comes in the bell

of illusion, the smell of jasmine

drifting in an incense-veiled bronze mirror.

"A zither, for no reason, has its fifty strings

broken. Across a stubble of pegs,

a cuckoo pecks for the lost years.

Tear-holding, a pearl appears sea-blued..."

What can be recaptured in memory

when it was lost then and there?

Master Zhuang awakes wondering

if it is he who dreamed

of being a butterfly, or if it is

a butterfly that dreams of being

Master Zhuang. Now the *zoom...zoom*

of the dryer she is applying to her hair

after the bath, or the distant sound

of guns the soldiers are firing

among the people in the square.

I begin making decisions: to go into exile,

not to compromise on the Chinese original,

to do justice to Li Shangyin. And she

comes to bed, turning off the light.

* Li Shangyin (813-858), a Tang dynasty poet, also Inspector Chen's favorite among the classical Chinese poets. Like other intellectuals at the time, Li went after an official position in the light of Confucianism, so as to serve his country. While a prominent poet, Li suffered devastating setbacks as a politician, which were often attributed to his marriage with Wang Yenmei, the daughter of an important member of the Li faction at the court. It was a move seen as of social climb by the rival Niu faction, which soon gained power. However, Li produced his best poems, often titled "Untitled," at the darkest moments in his official career. It's psychologically possible that while reading Li's poems, Chen sees a parallel in his own relationship with Ling.

Li Shangyin's English Version II

The fragrance of the jasmine in your hair

and then in my tea cup, that evening

when you thought me drunk, an orange

pinwheel turning at the rice-paper window.

The present is, when you think

of it, already the past. I am

trying to quote a line

from Li Shangyin to say what

cannot be said, but the English version

at hand fails to do justice

(the translator, drunk, divorced

from his American wife, found English

beating him like a blind horse),

as the micaceous mist rises

from a *Lantian* blue jade.

                    Last night's star,

last night's wind—the memory

of trimming a candle, the minute

of a spring silkworm wrapping itself

in a cocoon, when the rain

becomes the mountain, and the mountain

becomes the rain...

It is like a painting

of Li Shangyin going to open

the door, and of the door

opening him to the painting,

that Tang scroll you showed me

in the rare book section

of Beijing Library, while you

read my ecstasy as empathy

with the silverfish sleepy

in the eyes of the full stops.

And I felt a violent wonder

at your bare feet beating

a *Bolero* on the filmy dust

of the ancient floor. Even then

and there, lost in each

other's interpretations, we

agreed.

The horn is honking

outside the window. I am going

to a lecture on Lacan:

nothing but floating duckweed

of selves. Poetry makes

no jasmine petals fall.

An empty tea cup.

Restaurant Zen

comes in a Buddha's head carved out

of a white gourd, and steamed

on a willow-patterned platter.

Saw off a piece of the skull,

put your spoon into the brain,

and come up with a fried sparrow

inside a grilled quail inside

a braised pigeon inside a roast duck,

all saturated with the essence

of Zen.

A head is nothing

without other heads

stuffed inside.

* The special dish appears in *Red Mandarin Dress*.

Street Card Game

The card holds you,

the light focuses you,

the cigarette smokes you,

the moment seizes you...

You find and lose

yourself in what you do.

Watching, I become you,

the belt helplessly loosening...

* In the old city section where Chen grew up, people like to

engage themselves in games out on the street, with

surrounding onlookers. It's a scene not unfamiliar to Chen.

In Interpretation

Where else can we find ourselves

except in others' interpretations?

So you and I are framed

against a walnut tree whispering

in the wind, or a butterfly soaring

to the black eye of the sun...

Only by posing ourselves

in the proper light, and

the proper position,

can we be recognized as being

meaningful, the way a woodpecker

proves its existential values

from the echoes of a dead trunk.

Still, I am holding out to you

the bouquet of words blossoming

in your smile, and then

fading, like a see star drying

on a motel widow sill, leaving

water stains to interpretations.

* A slightly different version appears in *Don't Cry, Tai Lake*. At the beginning of the novel, Chen stays incognito by the lake, musing about identities in others' interpretations, writing the lines at random when he first meets with Shanshan.

Don't Cry, Tai Lake

She walks in a red trench coat

like a bright sail cutting

through the poisonous smog

enveloping the lake and its shore.

Amid chemical drops from a network

of corroded pipes overhead, long

in disrepair, a mud-covered toad

jumps upon the pollution report

in her hand, opening its sleepy eyes,

seeing all around still murky,

slumping back to sleep.

Who's the one walking beside you?

The broken metal-blue fingernails

of fallen leaves clutching

into the barren bank, the rotten fish

afloat on the water, shimmering

with their mercury-filled bellies,

their glassy eyes still flashing

the last horror at the apparition

of a black-bikinied witch dancing

with her raven hair streaming

on her alabaster shoulders, hopping

from the woods of the plant chimneys.

Who's the one walking beside you?

Terrible headache—

Go drink and forget about it—

You should see a doctor, young man.

But what's the point?

In the company production chart,

will your boss see the curve

of the production rising

or of the employees falling

with headache, herpes, and sickness?

Believe it or not, the pinnacle

of the cooling tower looks just

like the nipple of a sterile woman.

So tell me, where are you?

In Fortune Goddess' hair ribbon

or her itching crutch?

Who's the one walking beside you?

From the overpass of sound and fury,

you may see time flow like water

covered with dirty algae, empty can,

plastic bottles, cigarette butts, and what not.

Water has so many delusions

and cunning currents that deceive

with whispering ambitions and vanities.

If you are lost in the fantasies

of a solitary green reed swaying

in the wind, the water flows away,

leaving you behind, and you can't find

your way back. After so many years,

you still don't know?

Who's the one walking beside you?

A flash of her trench coat at dusk,

the water flowing like time,

and worries drifting like a boat.

A snatch of the violin melody

carried an elusive touch of deja vu

rippling in the Blue Danube,

so close, yet so far away. Here,

a water rat creeps out the slimy

ghastly green algae of toxic waste

spreading like omnipresent karma

for the immaculate purity

falsified in a tiny test tube.

Who's the one walking beside you?

Soon, the spring is departing again.

How much more of wind and rain

can it endure? The cobweb alone

seems to care, trying to catch

a wisp of the fading memories.

Why is the door always shut

covered in the dust of doubts?

A dog is barking in the cell

in the distance.

Who is the one walking beside you?

The moon startles up from a nightmare

immersed in ammonia, pale,

pensive in still speculation,

on its contaminated reflection

over the lake, the stars blinking

tearfully in the cold with the city

falling back asleep in cough,

and waking up in sneeze.

The siren, coming from afar,

shouts out terror through the night.

Another bottle of beer pops open,

bubble, bubble, bubble...

She pushes away the cup, walking

into the sour drizzle and twelve o'clock.

Who is the one walking beside you?

"Last night, a white water bird

flew into my dream again,

like a letter, telling me

that pollution's under control—

I awoke to see the night cloud

breaking through the ether, thinking

with difficulty, shivering,

as if the prison cell key was

heard turning only for once

before the door opens

to the anemic stars lost

in the lake of the waste..."

Who is the one walking beside you?

By the water, an apple tree

blossoming again, flashing

smiles among the waking boughs,

petal transparent in the dazzling light,

she walks in a red trench coat

carries a report in her hand

like a bright sail cutting

through the contaminated currents

to the silent splendid sun

* This is a poem Inspector Chen starts composing during an investigation by Tai Lake. It is a murder case in background of an environmental crisis. Through Shanshan, a learn environmental engineer, he comes to learn more about the pollution as well as the complicated social and political causes behind it. Inspired by Shanshan in her courageous battle for the environment, Chen dashes off lines, one or two stanzas at a time, at different stage of the investigation. The poem as presented in the novel *Don't Cry, Tai Lake* is not polished as Chen is too busy engaged in the murder investigation have time for revision. Also, it is because he tries to attempt the multi-voice-and-scene sequence like in The Waste Land, with a spatial structure too difficult for me in the middle of the murder case. The version here is one revised and rewritten after the conclusion of the investigation.

Immortality

They were talking on a balcony

over a waste of sand, sitting

in the shade of a blossoming iron tree.

She was wrapped in a white robe,

a blue starfish on her palm, breathing

out an invitation, still tangy, wet,

from the ocean. Autumn waves

in her eyes mirrored the response

he expected. The aquamarine fire

of the tiny points she moved

soft against his cheek.

The slippery intractable flesh

in flaming tongues called forth

a strange impulse. Exultant,

he put a bowl on a hot plate

recalling the secret of making

marine knickknacks a goggled diver

had taught them at the earlier tide.

Kicking off her slippers, kneeling,

she watched the starfish falling

into the bowl of steaming water,

splashing, starlit, infinite diamonds,

and writhing with its tentacles

straining up a greenish V

on the surface, like a pair

of ankles pointing to the sky,

the blue veins throbbing

with a gull's cry. She thought

of a man with a cloud of secretion

in his left eye watching

her undress, and she thrust

the surfacing tentacles down

with a chopstick.

A rain drop

fell on her brow. She awoke

to see a pale starfish

petrified by her side, its color drained

into the night. *It's ours*, he said.

Forever, she said. He tickled

her bare sole with its hardened points,

as if her glistening rounded toes

could keep the moment mothproof

like camphor balls. Reaching

for a kiss, he touched

the will-o'-the-wisp flickering

in her still wet hair.

A Bike Repairer Reading

Stretching himself

along a bamboo recliner

on the sidewalk, he has

the day's newspaper unfolding

overhead, like a hot towel

covering his face in barber shop,

smoothing out the deep lines

in the worry-etched forehead,

and then folding in the day.

What's happening in the world

happens only in the words.

On a worn-out tool table,

a time-yellowed sign declares,

"*bike-repairing, tire-fixing,*

and welding jobs too," a message

largely blocked by a black satchel,

and a pair of worn-out running

shoes. No business.

A city of bikes once, it is

lost, he reads, to cars.

The Moment of the River

Not the river, but the moment

of the river flowing into your eyes…

We stood at Huangpu Bridge, overlooking

a sampan tied to a stump swaying

under our gaze. A wave,

and a cloth diapers fell

from a clothesline across the deck.

"The future possibilities of the world

bob in a sampan cabin, " I said.

"A torn sail is married," you said,

outwitting me with a gum

on your tongue, "to an broken oar. "

A bubble of metaphor rose iridescent

in the sun. A naked baby crawled

out of the black tarpaulin mat

beneath us, as if born

of expectation. Reaching

into the imitation army satchel,

you produced the last apple

and tossed it to the newborn smile.

Two literature students, we had little,

but imagined the world

in the words

        At M on the Bund,

talking with Big Buck connections

over a Bloody Marry, I feel the hard

rock rolling the room like a sampan

in the river. A falling napkin

is reminding me of a letter to you

returned as "undeliverable" when

the restaurant is unexpectedly blacked out—

The light back, a blond waitress moves

over to the table in her heels, chewing

a gum with a colorful bubble

as glistening as before.

The wind blows us out,

a bubble of a dream.

* An imitation army satchel was considered fashionable in the seventies and eighties in China. "M on the Bund" is one of the most trendy restaurants in Shanghai. The restaurant boasts of a fantastic overview of the river, and sponsors the Shanghai International Writers' Festival, which Inspector Chen frequently attends.

Thoughts about Xue Tao

The man who marries Xue Tao

marries not a poet, nor poetry.

Not that she has to rhyme herself

through his breath, and to punctuate

her day and night following

his footsteps, but any new line

she writes, invariably, reminds him

of those written for other men, groaning

and moaning about the fantasies

of other nights. She dares not

to close her eyes when coming

least he suspects what's going

though her mind in the dark...

Even a kiss becomes a kitten

liable to scratch at the imagination.

* A Tang dynasty courtesan poet (768-832), well-known for her love poems. Little is known about her marriage, or the poems written by her afterward.

Trio

1. Tenor

Straw-stuffed, caught

in the rain, too saturated

to shake in the wind, to be

is to be constructed:

plastic buttons for your eyes

to keep the gray horizon

in a shroud of drizzling mist,

a carrot nose, half-

bitten by a mule, and

a broken ancient music box

for your mouth, wet,

eccentric, repeating

Ling-Ling-Ling

to the surrounding crows at dusk.

Setting afire a straw-yellow

photograph, murmuring, "Let bygones

be bygones," as if whistling alone

in the dark woods, I open

the window to the joyful sunlight.

Another day, when it begins to rain,

I am you again.

2. Alto

Stairs revolving slippers revolving stomachs

revolving springs revolving--

Oh in revolving I could hear

the word *Ling* whispered before dissolving

once again in a wisp of blue smoke

against the indifferent evening sky

over the Great Wall. He who's

on me becomes you.

A drunken swan flushes

out of the canvas, carrying

me to the ocean, where

the corals were my eyes shining

in yours. Missing your breath,

how can I feel the waves

seaweed-tangled, rising,

falling, and rising in me?

A blaze in the late autumn woods.

Dawn or dusk vomits blood again.

When you light the candles on a cake,

will you blow one out for me?

There is nothing

but in interpretation:

fallen maple leaves smolder

under a scarecrow's gaze.

3. Tenor & Soprano

Beside a wine barrel

a poster of Chinese virtues.

A smudge on the cheek,

my wife is peeling an orange

for a customer, wiping her hands

on a jasmine-embroidered apron.

"With such a family,

I dream no more dreams."

"No more dreams." I, too,

start nodding dutifully

into the poster, smiling

to the weather-beaten signboard--

Happy Family Restaurant

Washing possible recollections

from a greasy mop, I'm ladling

my fantasies out of the wok.

Day after day after day,

it breaths just with the little

freedom through a not-too-tightly

cocked bottle, issuing silence...

A recipe—put an ice cube

into the carp's mouth, fry it

for a second, add sauce, serve

with its eyes turning, turning...

"*Ling-ling*," somniloquous, I turn

to my alarmed wife, another night.

* After watching a Japanese movie named *Izakaya Choji*, Chen

wrote the poem, expressing himself dramatically through the

characters in the movie, in which a man runs a small pub with

his wife while unable to forget his first love. In Chen's lyrical

version, scenes are reset with Chinese details. The first part

"Tenor," though written earlier, appears in *Enigma of China*.

In front of a Seafood Eatery

The evening comes to life

in squirting clams, crowding squibs,

squirming trout, jumping frogs,

crawling crabs (as if still scuttling

across the silent bottom of the ocean

in dreams...) in the plastic basins,

with a snake-like hose dipping

in and out, busy pumping air

into a bubbling reality appearance

under the eyes of the likely

or unlikely customers standing

or squatting on the seafood-slippery street.

Six o'clock. A suckling baby scans

his mother's face framed

in the entrance under the flashing neon:

Private Room, Elegant Seat.

* A seafood eatery on Yunnan Road which is located

not far from Chen's old home. In his younger days, the

street was called "Junkyard Porridge Stalls," an echo from *The Story of a Red Lantern*, a Revolutionary Modern Beijing Opera in the Cultural Revolution; nowadays it is called "gourmet street" with an impressive facelift yet with some of its old stall-like features unchanged. The street appears in several Inspector Chen novels.

Bird Master

The little sparrow hops in

and out the tiny door

of the dainty bamboo cage,

parading about in dust,

with its wings so rigorously disciplined,

capable never more of flying,

but only flapping at the air.

A world of self-sufficient,

self-containing, barred enclosure—

with rice, water, vegetable,

and light, fresh air... enough

for its secured survival.

What's the point of breaking

out, alone, into the unknown?

Cheerful, it peeks back

to its old benevolent master

with his face shriveled

into a walnut of contented smile.

A flash of the sparrow's wing

in the light. History keeps

depositing into the forgotten corner

of the lane. What is meaningful

means only here and now,

in the little bird's ecstatic jump

under his blurred gaze.

Further down the lane,

a young couple are hugging

and singing: *Joy in your*

joy, pain in your pain...

* The scene, slightly modified, appears in *Shanghai*
Redemption.

Old Root

Old Root, a veteran of the "Red Dust Evening Talk," is sitting

out again in front of the lane, his glasses scintillating with the

lore of the ancient corner. Stripped to his waist, he crosses his

legs, one foot dangling over the cracked curb. Holding a

stainless steel cup above a concrete block, he readies himself

for the beginning of a story, quoting the lines from *The*

Romance of Three Kingdoms as a prelude.

The Yangtze River flows east,

pushing heroes through waves

upon waves—success or failure—

all gone in a flash.

The green mountains stand still,

like always, against the red sun

setting times and again.

By the river, a fisherman and

a woodcutter meet, having had

their days of the autumn moon,

spring wind, now both white-haired,

talking over a kettle of wine.

So many things, past

and present, are all rolling

into a tale full of laughter.

Behind Old Root, the peeling wall presents a fierce battle of

neighborhood ads for this brave new world: *sewer cleaning

13881938508, sewer cleaning 1352479264, sewer cleaning

13636593255, sewer cleaning and air conditioning installing

1991858*—the last two digits blocked by his clean-shaven

head, *hole-drilling* (what does that really mean?)—all the

digits after it blocked by his bare back.

* Among the old neighborhoods Chen likes to revisit, a

favorite one is Red Dust Lane. Particularly for the Red Dust

Evening Talk—a group of lane residents sit out in the evening,

telling stories and anecdotes in front of the lane, where Chen

used to go in his younger days. One of the regular story tellers

is a man nicknamed Old Root. For more information about

Red Dust Lane, you may find it in *Years of Red Dust.*

An Unworldly Peddler

Sitting at a small table

covered with bundles and

bundles of money, in millions

and billions, she is counting,

recounting bunches in dead

earnest, gazing ahead

at things invisible to others,

wearing a pair of polka dotted

over-sleeves for the job,

her elbows rubbing the edge

of the table non-stop, calculating—

richer than the wealthiest banker

in the world, all in cash,

for the underworld, shadows

and memories lurking around.

* It is conventional for Chinese people to burn the underworld

money in front of the grave, as if the dead could spend it there

under the ground. The scene, somewhat modified, is

represented in *Shanghai Redemption* during a visit Chen

makes to his father's grave in Suzhou.

Elegy

1

You had just said with a smile

the midnight siren was so charming,

so mysterious, when the window

opened, and dark torrents

tore the white pages

from your fingers.

2

No, I cannot forgive you:

in a trance of blazing poppies

against a cool moss-covered

shadow, you have forgotten

the night we spent on the bridge,

the light in the distance, and the lights

beyond them, converging

into music on your retina while

you conducted with a burning cigarette

a tone poem of the sleepless city,

and you no longer belonged

to a place, nor a time, nor yourself.

3

Now the ferries still ply

the neon-changing river,

swarthy sailors coiling the hawsers,

the boats so crowded, as always

the current so swift, the bells

so urgent, men hurrying

to destinations, and then

to new destinations, turning

on the shore to look back

at the one left behind,

still familiar, yet strange.

4

Oh, you should be there, still holding

the bow rail like a half-carved statue,

for the waves are always beginning,

beginning, and beginning again.

In the golden sunlight,

in the lemon-fragrant air

of another land, in the clear

water, you could have found

a new bronzed reflection.

5

A mast is passing my window

through the wind and rain,

and I am seeing you again

in the lightning across the dark,

your battered body reaching

out the rocks of contingency,

your lips covered with seaweeds

shivering in the stillness.

6

I understand, understand,

but a man is summed up,

after all, only in what

he has chosen to do—

the rest merely provides others

occasions for superfluous sighs.

When another white petrel flies

from the calendar, may you dream

no longer of a pale oyster

clinging to the grim limestone...

(Where are you now, as dawn taps

at the window with her rosy fingers,

as the fragrance of coffee and bread

penetrates the wakening mind,

and as the door, like a smile,

welcomes flowers and newspapers.

I will imitate your voice

on the telephone: "It is me!")

* It's written for one of Chen's friends in the early days.
Part of the poem appears in *Shanghai Redemption*
while Inspector Chen thinks about giving up his job.

Bubble of Wrigglers

Across the Song Dynasty bridge,

under the Tang Dynasty moon,

we are parting, like

the plum blossom folding

into a paper fan, like

the horizon sinking

on a crow's wing, as

the weeds start swinging

of a sudden,

to an unfamiliar tune.

Bubble of wrigglers

on the green water.

Chinese Chess

The bright moon of the Qing dynasty...

The ancient pass of the Han dynasty...

Soldiers after soldiers,

none of them ever returns

from the march, thousands

and thousands of miles long.

Oh that the winged general

of the Dragon City would still be here

to keep the Tartar horses

from crossing the Yin Mountains.

The Tang dynasty lines come

echoing, reverberating, clashing

over a chessboard still divided

with the Border of Kingdom Chu,

the Moat of Kingdom Han, where

you find that ancient world

of yours won and lost

through the battles raging

over the crisscrossing lines

on a worn-out stool shaking

in a time-forsaken corner.

The game over, you eye

each other, almost as ancient

in a sudden shaft of sunlight,

one stripped to the waste,

with the chest grooved like

an antique washing board,

the other in a motley pajama top

with un-matching pants,

silhouetted against the wall

crumbling with bullet-like holes.

* In the old neighborhoods of Shanghai, the scene of people

sitting out and playing the Chinese chess is one familiar to

Chen. It is a popular ancient game with the chess board made

of the dividing line "The Moat of Kingdom Chu" and "The

Border of Kingdom Han." The stanzas in the Italic echo from

a poem by Wang Changling (698-757), a well-known Tang

dynasty poet.

Karma

Despite the superstitious commandment

that you shall not walk under the wet clothing—

particularly, the woman underwear—dripping

from the bamboo poles crisscrossing

the patch of the sky over the alley,

what can a poor old man do

but to move in and out, sneaking

under them, shuffling, shivering

with a cold drop on his head, leaning

on a cracked cane? Born and grown up

in this narrow alley, having to enter

and exit here day in and

day out, little wonder

a loser in the end.

Poetry

Back home at 8:30

with five or six small fish

in the pail, including

a baby blue gill, which

should not have been counted,

a water snake, with its triangular head

smashed into a rotten persimmon—

still, not a too bad day, I have

to say, a sunburned nose

peeling, puckered up

in a pleasant smile

under the scrutiny of my wife,

who, seeing on my bare back

a map of mosquito bites, snaps:

What's the point—nine hours

under the scorching sun, you have

to buy the gasoline, the drink, the bait,

two hot dogs, half a pack of China, and

now with the pathetic fish, three or four yuan

at the most in a market, you are really hooked.

She is an accountant. No point

calculating a split-second

of catching the golden sun

in silver scales.

Don Quixote in China

Once more, you are going to mount the bony horse,

old, tired, dispirited, like yourself.

A cloud of dust rises on the road.

Nothing but dust, but you

uphold your shield, as if it were

the setting sun over an ancient empire.

In a bronze reflection

you discover a broken figure identifiable

only in the shape of a rusty suit

of armor that keeps you going, too

busy going to recognize yourself.

Absurd or not, what choice do you have?

A role played too long, inevitably,

plays you. You dare not

to lie under the ash tree, or

doubts, like termites, will rush

to hollow your trunk.

What shines, you cover your eyes

with the back of your hand, shines

in your mind alone.

Dear Sancho,

dumb, dutiful as ever, shoulders

a newly fixed lance, looking

up at you, waiting.

He, too, has to find himself

in something he is capable

of doing, dragging his feet

along the unfamiliar road, wandering

in your company.

59652956R00079

Made in the USA
Charleston, SC
12 August 2016